NOMADS 3

Carol Bergman

Nomads 3

Copyright © 2016 by Carol Bergman

mediacs@gmail.com (646) 216-9246

A *Mediacs* Publication

/MEDIACS

Cover design Copyright © 2016 by Chloe Annetts
www.chloeartdesign.com

Cover photograph by Carol Bergman

for the next generation

Henry, Javi, Carla, Ella, Harvey, Noah,
Dylan, Wesley, Thea, Zoe, Ridley,
Luca x2, Cora, Ellis, Pearl Rose and Mila

may they grow up in a kinder, safer
and more peaceful world

A NOTE FROM THE AUTHOR

The idea of a finished picture is a fiction.
—Barnett Newman

This is an unfinished work of fiction. The "I" in some of the stories is not the author, or it may resemble the author. The narrative persona may be a woman, or it may be a man, or it may be a person of indeterminate gender and age, or an omniscient reporter who knows everything, or nothing. Usually nothing.

The reader, on the other hand, opens the book and becomes, at once, a collaborator in the creation of the book. Once they are read, the words and sentences resonate like obsessive internal chatter.

1. THE LOVE SONGS OF GULLS

BEACH MEMORY

The sand had never been so hot, the air so dry. It was windy, the waves were high. He was lying face up on the blanket, his hat pulled over his eyes. She was standing, restless, casting a shadow onto his torso. The smell of oil and salt and sea. Half past one. Her thoughts sputtered and she said, "Let's swim." She reached for his arm and pulled it up. "Get up," she said. He laughed and pulled her down. His hat blew off. "Shit," he said as he drew her into his chest. The future opened: their love would fade. It was already half-buried in the dune.

INCUBATOR BABY

Even a baby has a story. She had been taken down for x-rays and was wrapped up inside the incubator, a little hat on her head, a striped blanket covering her and oxygen pumping through a tube into her nose. Such a small little baby. There were two nurses with stethoscopes around their necks, one on each side of the incubator. A priest was standing next to them, and when the elevator arrived, everyone gave way for the procession: two nurses, the baby inside the incubator, the priest. "This baby gets right of way," I said. Where were her parents? How could they have let their baby out of their sight? Why did she need an x-ray? I began to cry, just a soft, whispering cry. Then everyone in the elevator fell silent. The priest raised his finger and pressed it against the glass near the baby's head. He said a blessing. "This baby needs to be blessed," the priest said. So we all blessed the baby.

CYCLADIC WOMEN

Even though they felt like dancing, they were not permitted to dance. They were not only posed in the workshop, they were posed at the well, at the communal table, in the marriage bed. After a while their crossed arms automatically assumed the correct position under their breasts, the right above the left, a natural corset. Their breasts were bare, their navels exposed above wrapped linen skirts. The fabric fell to their ankles. Their foreheads were shaved exposing their aquiline faces to the sun. Their eyes drooped modestly.

HE WAS EATING A GOAT'S NECK

It was very dark and I couldn't see the room in its entirety. A man was sitting at a table with a tankard in front of him. It could have been cider or beer. There was no wine in this establishment, a crude way-station on the way north. Horses were tethered at the back, on the side, and at the front. The roof sloped onto a decrepit drain, water dripping incessantly onto the stoop.

It had been a cold autumn. I was traveling on my own dressed as a man, escaping from the man I was supposed to marry; a dowry had been raised and presented.

I paid my two pence, dragged myself up the stairs, stashed my belongings, and returned to the main room for vittles. I asked what the man was eating and said I would have the same, tankard and all. But when it arrived, the odor was overwhelming. A goat's neck filled with nourishing marrow, the proprietor said. Would you have some potatoes? I asked. It was all I could stomach.

MR. VENDEM

A young girl lives in the woods far away from a construction site. The site has not always been there; it's new. Say an oil company has arrived or gold diggers from Alaska or diamond miners from South Africa. Say a pipeline is going to be built without regard for the villages or people in its path.

It's a warm sunny summer day and the child has been instructed by her mother to go to the store. All she wants to do is to return home quickly to play with her friends.

She's walking along at a brisk pace through the woods onto the dirt road when she hears machinery. Further along, she can see mechanical shovels and bull dozers. Further still, there is large sandy pit where the road used to be. She stops.

She walks to her left and then to her right searching for a path around the pit. She steps over rusty pipes and granite rocks. A man calls a warning to her. Get away, he says. The road is closed.

She sits down on the hard rocky ground. At least it's dry, she thinks to herself, grateful for once that there has not been a lot of rain. Then she moves closer to the pit and dangles her thin legs and bare feet over the edge. Finally, a big burly dark-skinned man wearing a bright red hard hat comes over to her. He asks her gently if she'd like some help. She explains that she is supposed to walk to the village to order supplies.

The man lifts her up and carries her to the other side of the pit. He's Mr. Vendem he tells her, better known as her Knight in Shining Armor. Mr. Vendem, she says. You are my Mr. Vendem.

And from then on, the young girl dreamt about him and hoped one day to marry him.

He was tall and slim, wearing a black jacket. And though his hair was dyed black with gray showing at the roots, he was ageless, like other angels I have met.

I WISH TO SAY

I wish to say that today is William Shakespeare's birthday. I am married to his mind in so many ways. As a compass turns, I turn with his every mood. If I am wrong, please correct me. Oh, no, I am not wrong, then let me continue before it is too late. And if I overstay my visit, feel free to remove me. I cannot alter my devotion or bend to anyone else's desires. It is Shakespeare I love. His worth is known to me and I will not damage his esteem of me. As for time's rosy lips that take me to the pinnacle of life, the very doom of existence shall sickle me. Oh, no, let me continue to write forever more in Shakespeare's presence with his every breath enlivening me.

A THRILLING AFTERNOON
WITH A GORILLA

I would like to report my afternoon at the zoo which began Friday last at approximately 11 a.m. I entered at the south gate and proceeded immediately to the "Congo Enclosure." I am happy to report that the guerrillas, as opposed to the gorillas, were in retreat. This was not planned or scheduled *per se*, but I had it in mind that it would be my first port of call, so to speak. On the way I passed one skinny tiger and two leopards. All three were pacing restlessly in their habitats. The four full-grown gorillas, on the other hand, were serene. Two of them were sleeping, one was searching for scraps of kale the keepers had provided, and a very large male came right up to the glass barrier. Was this normal? What would happen if the barrier broke? Of course it was enchanting to be so close to this wonderful creature. And he probably felt the same, don't you think? Because we are also enchanting creatures, are we not? We humans, I mean.

We "communicated" for several minutes eye to eye, pointed finger to pointed finger. The crowd around me was sweating. There was a strong smell, not of the gorillas, but of the humans gawking at the gorillas—myself included. The air was tropical, dense and unventilated. I thought I might faint, and when I came to, I had an epiphany: we were all imprisoned in this habitat together. The glass barrier was an illusion. Inside, outside, it made no difference. We had done this to the gorillas and to ourselves.

AND THIS IS MY ROAD

And this is my road. And this is my undulating road. And these are the turning leaves. And this is the unbroken road. And up ahead is the fork in the road. And this is the white line that looks like a skunk's back. The horizon. The clouds. The mountain, all this is mine. I can see it all from the road as I walk on the road. This is the road I have taken. And this is the road I have not taken. And this is the bend in the road. Beyond the trees are houses and people inside their houses and on their porches, a child on a tire swing, another playing ball. Beyond the trees and houses is a pond and a farm. Chickens, rabbits and pigs, vegetables, bats and mice, a family of bears, toads in the pond, chipmunks, a dog, a cat. And this is my road, my beautiful undulating road.

LEARNING TO DRIVE

My longing to drive was like a constant fever. My father let me take the wheel on a country dirt road and, later, in a parking lot. I was only fifteen but tall enough to look older. I could see over the wheel which helped. I wasn't afraid. I couldn't believe my luck. I wanted to drive all across the country and never stop. One day, I told my dad to get out of the car so I could see what it felt like to drive alone. He agreed and I took off, out of the parking lot, back onto the dirt road which led to the parkway, left signal on and off I went. He called the cops and they chased me for about ten miles. I wasn't going fast, only about 50 mph or so, but they didn't want to startle me into an accident. I was so self-assured, never for a minute did I think I'd have an accident. They gave me a stern warning and started laughing. They thought it was the funniest damn thing that a fifteen-year-old in pigtails had stolen her father's car. Little did they know what it meant to me.

ALEXI'S JOURNEY ACROSS UNKNOWN CONTINENTS

Alexi has arrived in the city on horseback after many years of travel. He has long thick black hair and his body is lithe and strong. He is barefoot, nude from the waist up, sun-streaked, and hungry.

The year is 1510 BCE, the city is Alexandria. And though he has followed the stars, he does not know where he is. Perhaps at the edge of the world?

He follows the aroma of baking bread into a shop and holds out his hand like the beggars he has seen on the streets as he entered the city. They were either sitting cross-legged or sitting on their haunches. They reminded him of the animals in the forest. Some were moving among the crowds, their begging cups jangling with coins.

A young woman in the bakery stopped what she was doing and went to speak to her mistress in the back of the shop. *There is a man*, she said. The mistress came out to look at him. Alexi smiled.

It didn't take long for a crowd to gather. This man, was he a spy or simply a wanderer in search of destiny? Where were his clothes? Where had he come from? If they allowed him to remain in the city, what would become of him? What would become of them if he returned to his kingdom and reported their wealth and well-being?

Alexandria was a model of enlightenment in those days. Rather than kill the traveler or imprison him, they put him to work in the bakery and gave him a storage room to sleep in. Eventually, he found a woman, had children, grew old, and died peacefully in his adopted city.

HOW THE CONVERSATION ENDED

A man and a woman are spending the afternoon together at a museum. It will be their last afternoon together for a while, or perhaps forever.

They meet at 3:30 p.m. They are always both on time and this last time is no different. They check their bags, pay, and enter. The man is wearing a colorful short-sleeved shirt. The woman is wearing long earrings. They do not comment on their attire, their appearance, or anything about their personal attachment; they are focused on the art.

Some of the portraits are very large, some are smaller, all are of noble men and women in the 17th century Dutch court. Most are wearing starched millstone collars, an emblem of prosperity.

"How uncomfortable they must have been," she says.

He does not agree or disagree. He walks away with his hand to his chin, or both hands behind his back.

They stroll onto the avenue to look for a café. It is the first warm day of summer.

"I do not want to walk far," she says.

She orders a latte, he orders a glass of wine.

"Don't worry, I'm not going to disappear," he says.

"But you have sold everything," she reminds him. "Even your television set."

EATING PRUNES

She had just arrived from Monaco and was on the terrace eating prunes. He was behind the wicker settee sitting cross-legged, meditating, oblivious to her arrival. She had been preparing a speech during the journey home and had even written it out several times. A declamation as much as a declaration, she thought to herself. She would ask him to listen without interrupting her.

How poetic it was, her longing for him. How persistent and inexplicable. He was not worthy. He was not even there in the corporeal sense.

You can't do this to me, she began. She had the urge to touch the top of his head. It took her only a few moments to realize the futility of the gesture and she withdrew her hand before it touched him.

This wasn't love, it was a fantasy. He was a canvas on which she had painted her life.

A LOVE STORY ABOUT A BOW
FOR MF

First, the musician chooses the not yet endangered Brazilian permambuco wood. He has rejected the snake wood. He has rejected the synthetic carbon. He holds the permambuco vertically and strokes it north to south. He holds it to his ear. He says to the bow maker: This is my wood. I can hear the rainforest in this wood.

Then the bow maker says: I have a horse's tail from Siberia. I will make you this bow.

And the musician says: I have to like the bow and the bow has to like my cello, and when I place the bow upon my cello, the cello and the bow have to sing to me.

MY LITTLE ORPHAN BOY

Don't be angry if he doesn't listen to you, they said. He won't listen to you. Reduce your breathing to 4-6 breaths per minute. Chant, if necessary: *My little orphan boy. My little orphan boy.* You have adopted this child at two. And there have been rumors from whence he came. Rumors, not facts. One can only imagine.

After a while—and one does not know how long—there will be adjustments, there will be understanding. Eventually, there will be love.

AFTER THE WEDDING

Say, for example, we are attached to someone of the same gender and then this person marries someone of the opposite gender. We assume it has nothing to do with us, it is for appearance only, for the sake of career advancement, or the reputation of a family that cares about such things. There has been no explanation, only an announcement, and then an invitation to the wedding itself.

How are we to dress? Will we be able to smile? To dance? To offer our hand in congratulation to the fortunate bride, to hug our special friend and whisper into his ear: I shall miss you.

HE'S SO SWEET
for Dolly Parton

He's so lovely, he's so sweet, he's my honey, he's so neat. He's my angel, he's my love, he's my lover, he's my dove.

He's so lovely, he's so sweet, he's my honey, he's so neat. He's my he-man, he's my love, he's so special, he's my dove.

He's so lovely, he's so sweet, he's my honey, he's my love, he went roaming in the cove.

I'm so bitter, I'm so blue, I can't figure out what's true.

ARE YOU SEXY?

What I need is an answer, he said. Are you sexy?

How should I know, I said.

I didn't like his voice. It was hoarse, demanding, over-confident.

If you aren't sexy, why should I be interested?

I don't care if you are interested or not, I said. I am doing this for the money. College loans. If you like my picture and my profile, I'll come over. I can't stay on the phone much longer.

10 p.m., he said. Then he gave me the address. Take a cab, he said. Put it on my bill.

It was in an upscale neighborhood north of Georgetown. The lights were on in every room. Secret Service at the door, two men, straight as poles, ear pieces, gray suits, dark blue ties.

They opened the door without even one question. No credentials. No proof of anything. They didn't search my bag. I could have been anyone, an assassin even.

They'd had instructions, he told me. Let her in. She's a friend of my daughter's.

LOL, I was the same age as his daughter!

You mean to tell me the Secret Service didn't know he was alone? That his daughter and his wife were traveling somewhere? Even I knew that. I watch the news.

It was just ordinary, boring sex. I don't know why he bothered, why he took the risk.

But he did.

WHY DOES HE ALWAYS WEAR BLACK?

A black turtle neck, black slacks, this is his uniform, day in and day out. In summer it's black T-shirts and black linen pants, always black, drowning in black. His house is bare of furniture, the fridge is empty. In the freezer, a few items: not food, but toys. Scrabble tiles in a hand-crocheted sack (stiff from cold), a plastic dildo (stiffer from cold). She asks if he'd like to play. What? he asks. Both, she says.

In the living room there are choices: free-standing designer chairs (three of them) and a 1950's barely upholstered black sofa. She suggests they sit side by side. Are you ready to make love? she asks. Or would you rather place a letter on the board? There's no board, he says.

They walk to the window arm in arm. They are high up and the sunlight at this altitude is blinding. She leans into him. There is no resistance, neither is there any encouragement.

SEDUCED BY A FOUNTAIN PEN

They were at a party sitting around a low coffee table filled to overflowing with food. Their host was Armenian, a very good cook. And then there was the booze, everyone well lubricated, and the exotic music, a few people dancing. San Francisco. The 1990's. A mixed crowd.

He took out his fountain pen, unscrewed the top, and asked if she had a piece of paper. "Is that a real Montblanc?" She had never owned a Montblanc, had never known anyone who did. She handed him a small notebook she kept in her purse, spiral bound.

"There's a book I want to tell you about," he said. "I'll write down the title. While I'm doing that you can give me your phone number."

This wasn't a request. He didn't ask permission. He just took the number down as though it had always belonged to him. She watched the blue-black ink slide out of the nib, like blood exiting a vein.

A week later he invited her to dinner. He didn't care that she was married. And she didn't either, apparently, because she said yes. She told her husband and he was amused.

"But he didn't invite you," she said.

"It doesn't matter," he said.

So she went.

She didn't like the food or the pretentious waiter with his long list of specials. But the man—this man, this strange man— seemed to enjoy it all. Why had he invited her? Why had she accepted?

Then, at one point, during a lull in the conversation, she asked to borrow his Montblanc pen. With a flourish, she took out her spiral notebook and added a few items to her shopping list.

THE DIVINE SARAH

The most famous actress the world has ever known stepped into the vertical railroad at The Players Club in New York on November 10, 1890. This was, and still is, a one-person elevator with red walls and a small gate that the passenger must close herself from inside.

Why didn't The Divine Sarah walk up the stairs? It was a beautiful carpeted staircase leading from the ground level to the fourth floor. But her manager had said, "You are tired my dear, take the lift." He was British so the word he used to describe the new contraption was "lift."

The Divine Sarah stepped into the lift and was instructed by the concierge: "Close the gate, Madam," and he demonstrated with a theatrical gesture in her honor.

But the gate was not entirely closed. The elevator moved and then it stopped between floors. The Divine Sarah began to swear and shout. "This is a good opportunity to practice your English," her manager said.

The Fire Department was called. They arrived *post haste*, but when they discovered the object of the rescue, they became oddly paralyzed. It was almost an hour before The Divine Sarah was released from captivity. Feeling only slightly woozy, she decided to feint a faint.

The next day, the incident was reported in the newspapers: "I was in utter despair, weeping bitter tears that stained my cheeks," The Divine Sarah said.

And everyone believed her.

THE EMPRESS DOWAGER CIXI

Her body is her minaret, her throne a bird, the chamber pot a gilded scented lemon. Visitors to the court are not permitted to sit, they must stand. All the doors are open to the manicured gardens, etched in stone and hibiscus. A shrine with baby shoes, baby hair, discarded buttons and zippers, emblems of Mongolian ancestry and imperial prowess. Her feet, unlike the Mandarin ladies in her court, remain unbound.

WHO DO YOU THINK YOU ARE?
in memory of Malick Sidibé

A woman with a flower. *La femme avec un fleur.* I prefer it in French, he says. *La femme avec un fleur.*

At each session, he asks, "Who do you think you are?" He likes to see his models dance. When we dance we express who we really are. "What is real about you?" he asks.

Here, for example, is a man who drives a taxi, a taximan. *Taximan avec voiture.* He stands next to his vehicle, an extension of his very self.

The stars belong to you, he says of his models, especially when we are young, especially when we dance.

THE MAN WHO BLEW ME A KISS

I was in a cafe in Vila Nova De Milfontes. It faced the sea and it was dusk. And though the sky is beautiful everywhere, it was particularly golden that warm summer evening in Portugal. I was there on holiday and I was alone, looking for holiday love.

The cafe was crowded. In fact, there was only one seat available at a table near the floor to ceiling glass window. A man was sitting there. I couldn't see his face but from the back he looked handsome. He sat straight, had a full head of hair and a long torso. I like tall men.

I am not usually a bold woman but on holiday I try to reinvent myself. No one I know from home is there to observe or criticize. I can be a vamp if I wish. I can dress any way I please. I let the circumstance and my mood guide me.

I approached the table and sucked in my breath. "May I share the table with you, Senhor?"

I spoke in English; I cannot speak Spanish or Portuguese though I should know Spanish by now as I am from New York. But I don't.

The man turned his head towards me—I was now standing on his left—and gestured for me to sit down. He was old. An old man with a young, upright body. I had not expected this and, needless to say, I was disappointed. I called for the waiter and put the novel I was reading on the table. Would I be able to concentrate? The man watched me intently. He had deep-set eyes, a scraggly beard, and weatherworn skin. A fisherman perhaps? His small straw hat was turned upside down in front of him. His clothes were soiled and he looked like a beggar.

I was absorbed in my novel when the waiter returned with my coffee. The old man was mute and I remained mute in his presence. I very much wanted to be sitting at another table but I also did not want to be rude. So I continued reading and sipping on my coffee. The man had nothing in front of him but his upturned straw hat.

Several minutes passed. I looked up and he was still watching me intently. The waiter came over and put his hand on the man's shoulder. "Pai," I heard him say. That much I could understand. This man was his father. Were they talking about me? "Are you talking about me?" I asked the waiter. And I pointed to myself. Oh, it was a great misunderstanding. The old man reached over the table with one of his rough hands. And with the other he blew me a kiss. He blew me a kiss! I couldn't believe it. Even worse, everyone in the cafe was looking at me and laughing.

THE WEEK THE CAT DISAPPEARED
That feral, feisty cat, so loved

When should we stop calling for her? When should we stop looking for her? When should we put away her food, dump her litter, toss her bed? When should we sweep up all the cat hair, get out the vacuum cleaner? When should we take down the signs?

What if we find her body on the road, or in the woods, or splayed on the electric fence? What if she suffered? What if she called out to us with her insistent meow?

When will we stop imagining her appearance on the stoop at supper time or first thing in the morning? When will her presence become a memory? When will we begin to talk about her in the past tense? When will our grief subside? When will we be able to post a eulogy on Facebook? When should we get a new kitten?

WISH YOU WERE HERE

What stirs me is the small stories they tell, the careful handwriting and the salutations: dearest, dear, with love, with everlasting affection, and so on. I have never received or sent any postcards like those I collect, nor am I nostalgic for any trips I have taken to faraway places such as Niagara Falls, for example. There was no one in my life at the time I wanted to write to about my trip. I just went, enjoyed the falls, talked to one or two people, and came home.

So it confounds me that people would document their trips with a postcard to friends and relatives. Why bother when they will only end up at a thrift store or in my house?

WINTER MEMORY

The school year began: new crayons, notebook, lunchbox, pens and pencils, a pencil case, new shoes (we'd grown, we were spurting), hems down on our dresses, new dresses, a new winter jacket.

It was just weeks before the first puff of cold air, gloves and snowflakes, bells on our shoelaces. We didn't own dolls, or maybe just one or two decoratively placed on a shelf above our beds. We read comics, watched "The Lone Ranger," ice skated once or twice a week. It was cold, biting. We skated anyway.

I remember the sleds, too, wooden with metal blades, the snow packed thick enough to create a cushion, snow piled on top of cars up to the back window, snow days without a mayor's equivocation—should we or shouldn't we shut the schools?

COWS

I walked down the cow path early in the morning. It had rained and the smell of hay and dung was sweet. There were butterflies and bluebells to keep me company, otherwise I was alone for a while. I heard their bells approaching and picked up my pace. I didn't want to walk with the cows that morning, or next to them, or behind them. I had just released them into the pasture and was headed home for breakfast. I would see them again at day's end and spend more time.

They followed me. They had started doing this of late, it was instinctual. No matter how busy I was, I needed them— their hot breath, their sweet eyes—and, miraculously, they sensed my need.

I walked slowly as they approached and turned. They were of varying colors: brown and black and white. They were large long-haired cows with a rolling gait. Some of them had just calved, others were still pregnant. The sight of them made me smile.

They ambled gently to the edge of the path and stopped. They stood in a line, one after the other waiting for my command to enter the path.

2. WHAT DID YOU EXPECT
WOULD HAPPEN?

FEELING THE KILL

It was five years after the end of the Civil War and two of the neighbors had been Union soldiers. They had wives and children, animals, shelter, food and a community of neighbors helping one another to return to. In all this, they were blessed.

On that hot July morning one of the black barn cats had escaped onto the road and the rabbits were eating their breakfast with gusto like prisoners downing their last supper and the rooster was hooting incessantly and the ducks were in and out of the pond and the dogs were chasing them. The orchard was nearly complete with a grape arbor and fruit trees, a blueberry patch and clover field for the bees.

The kill station had been set up at the far end of the property and the rabbits, one by one, were brought there for slaughter. Six neighbors were there to to help and they prayed and blessed the rabbits and thanked them.

But that night at dinner, the neighbors gathered to partake of their bounty, the rabbits roasting on an open fire, something was different. One of the soldiers—his name was Jack—put down his fork. He looked at the meat and saw before him the torn, singed flesh of his fallen comrades and he smelled the rotting flesh of their wounds.

I CAN'T BELIEVE THEY'RE GONE

Every so often, usually when I am cooking or washing the dishes or making the beds or cleaning the bathroom—and why then, just at those moments, I have no idea—I think about the people I've known and loved who are gone.

Oh, I think, as I am watering the plants, I can't call my mother today, she's not there. Or my friend, Dan. An illness took him too young. I can still hear him playing the jazz piano—by ear, he couldn't read notes. I want to call to tell him how much I love Bill Evans these days, but he's gone, and I can't call him. (And Bill Evans is gone, too.)

And what about my brother who is still very much alive but won't talk to me. What about him? And should he even be included in this story?

And what about me? Will there be someone—anyone— somewhere in the future who will think about calling me and then remember that I am gone?

MY VOICES
for S

I lie awake in the cool darkness and pray that they have not followed me here. I am secluded in this house, all doors and windows locked, a knife under my pillow. But if they find me, I will surrender.

My voices tell me they will arrive by boat. They will be well armed; my knife will be useless. I will not recognize them and I will not understand their language. My cat will flee into the rafters.

I have not eaten for several days. Messages arrive as I sleep and I have been afraid to drive to town for provisions. They have poisoned the water. Once it is dark, I walk through the high grass to the lake and fill a small bucket with water. I drain it, then boil it. So far I have not been sick. But I am hungry.

What will they do to me if I am captured? If I could imagine my captivity I might feel safe again. Imagination is anticipation, is it not? They will arrive, they will shackle me and they will take me away. I will spend the remainder of my life in the bosom of my tormentors.

NON FINITO
inspired by Colm Tóibín's "Brooklyn"

Homeward bound. Just because she is returning does not mean the story is finished or that the canvas of her life is complete. There are more years ahead, for which she is grateful. She is still young. She has remained healthy despite her ordeal.

She did not get sick on the return voyage. Outbound, she had filled a bucket with vomit. The solution was obvious: do not eat.

It wasn't only the roiling ship, it was her fright and her sorrow. Her mother and sister had waved to her from the dock. This parting was too hard to bear.

The man who waited for her in San Francisco shook her hand, picked up her suitcase and steered her, his hand on the small of her back, to his car. There was a driver. It appeared that he had been telling the truth in his letters: he was rich.

Her uncle had arranged this marriage. It was forbidden in America which meant nothing. If she was asked, her answer—in halting English—would be, "Yes this is my husband." She had memorized his name, his origins, his occupation, where they would live.

It took her a year to find the courage to escape. In truth, the man was kind enough, at times. But as soon as she saw him, she knew she would not stay.

NOTICE OF A DATA BREACH

We would like to make sure you have the facts about what happened and what steps we are taking to protect your savings. Shortly before Christmas—and we apologize for taking such a long time to inform you—we noticed that our data had been stolen. All our data, including yours. Our CEO has already re-settled in Greenland with his cat and, for the moment, is unreachable. In fact, everyone on our team is unreachable. We no longer have an email address or 800 telephone number. We have closed down our offices.

We would like to reassure you that this is an ongoing international investigation. When it is complete someone—and we cannot say who this will be—will contact you.

MEMORABILIA

There were secret sanctuaries. They realized this as soon as they entered the house after her death. Boxes inside boxes, folders inside folders, a hidden panel in the guest room closet. They pried it open easily with a fork. "Not that hidden," the lawyer said. The locks had been changed. They had not been allowed onto the premises unless the lawyer was present. And that was a shock, one among many.

The will was in dispute. Various paintings had been designated for this person or that. Furniture to Goodwill. Books to the local library. The piano to a favorite grandchild. There were two children—sons—and each of them had two children. And they were already arguing when, suddenly, a half-sister appeared. Due diligence, she had been found.

She had been living in Rio for three decades. This was the disappeared child, the abandoned child, the one who had been given away. Pregnancy, adoption and suddenly this heir appears, the lawyer explained. "Stand down. All will be resolved during probate. You cannot claim anything," she told the two sons.

These two brothers were as different as pie and cheese. One was mostly interested in old photographs, the other in the valuable paintings, furniture and a crystal collection.

Both of them hated their mother; she had a dry heart. After their father died, if they saw her once a year, it was too much. Neither did they enjoy one another's company. And now they were at each other's throat, an accurate description of inheritance disputes. Not a cliché at all.

The missing sibling arrived from Rio and arranged to meet the lawyer at the house, which had become a "premise," the premise being that the lawyer would have to decide everything. She unlocked the door: everything but the kitchen had been stripped bare.

"Now my work really begins," said the lawyer, and she called the cops. They arrived and took a report. But before any investigation began, the two brothers met with the lawyer. They had divided the spoils between them and had no interest in meeting their sister. They refused to return anything to the house.

"Breaking and entering," the lawyer said. "To what end?"

"Memorabilia," the brothers explained, almost as one person.

But of course that was not the end of the story, it never is. A court date was set, the discarded sister returned from Rio. This was more than three years later. In the meantime, the house had been sold, the proceeds placed in escrow. It just about covered the lawyer's bills.

FRIEND INVENTORY IN THE AGE OF ELECTRONIC MEDIA

It's my birthday week and I am taking an inventory of my friends. This is probably not a good idea but I can't resist. I've done it before, years ago, when I was "transitioning" as they say—they meaning me-psychology pundits—from one job to another, from one country to another, and from one steady relationship to no relationship at all. The list was long; I left many friends behind on another continent. And I wept as I wrote the list. We stayed in touch for a while, these friends and I, via phone calls and long letters and the occasional visit.

This time no transitioning, just the usual self-pity during my birthday week. Who loves me? Who will remember me? Will my snail mailbox be empty? Will my email mailbox be filled with junk and trash or will there be some happy bappy electronic greeting cards? Will I get any phone calls or texts or Facebook messages? Will anyone offer to take me out to lunch? Why do I miss my long-dead lover? What kind of inventory is this?

I have already decided what I am going to say on my Facebook page: Thanks for your happy birthday greetings. Please call me. I miss your voice. If you are nearby, let's get together.

ARE YOU A GRANNY?

Sometimes strangers ask me if I am a granny. I'm not a granny but even if I were a granny I wouldn't want to be a granny. Grannies are old. I am not old. Grannies are retired. I am not retired. Grannies are not interested or curious or fit. I am interested and curious and fit. Also, I have a name. Whoever you are, please call me by my name. That name has been with me all my life, and although it is not what I might have chosen, there's worn callous around it, like a rock.

Look at me stranger. Look into my eyes. Ask me questions about my life and what I'm doing right now. Never mind how old you think I am or where I should be in my life based on how old you think I am or what my relationship is to the person who is introducing us. Don't get glazed over with expectation when you see my silver hair which, by the way, is fashionably silver and pretty damn gorgeous if I do say so myself. Get to know me. Don't assume anything.

AN ARGUMENT IN FAVOR
OF BEHEADINGS

Beheading with a sword goes back a long way in history because, like hanging, it was both cheap and practical and, let's be frank, a sword was always readily available. For these very reasons—the availability, the cheapness, the practicality—we should approve of this form of execution and write it into law once again. I speak for my constituents in this matter. Many have petitioned me in recent months. Simple, clean, fast, no apparatus required other than the sword, available in every household, as I have said.

Some more historical context: Beheading cont-inued in Britain up to 1747 and was the standard method in Norway (abolished 1905), Sweden (abolished 1903) and Denmark (abolished 1892). It was used for some classes of prisoners in France until the introduction of the guillotine in 1792 and in Germany up to 1938. We all know what happened after that: chimneys.

As for the Chinese, they replaced beheadings with shooting—also fast, but the equipment required is both expensive and difficult for some to handle. Considering the volume of guns in the United States, however, shooting might still be preferable to beheading in some states.

Madam Chairwoman, I yield my time.

AN ADVERTORIAL

I don't recall what final insanity drove me away or what season it was when I began to watch television all day long, the sound and images like wallpaper in my room. It was one room, my only room, all my distilled possessions stuffed into three drawers, one small closet, and a desk. I piled my remaining books on the desk and the rickety bedside table. I didn't have trouble giving things away. I like to give things away and see the joy on someone's face as they receive an unexpected gift, a piece of jewelry, for example. I know what my friends like, what they covet. I had no desire for anything sparkly or joyous. I had to find joy elsewhere, in the giving itself, in the sunrise. I was grateful I could sleep through the night.

My cousin had taught me how to sing so I began to sing pop songs as they played on the radio. The air whistled through my teeth. My boots were warm. I was grateful for that, too. The television worked, the cable was free. I was glued to Dr. Oz who had advice for me about staying healthy, slim and positive. I couldn't figure out where the advice ended and the ads began. Maybe they were one and the same.

One morning I woke up crying, I remember that now. At least you are feeling something, I said to myself. I was relieved and, once again, grateful, that I could still feel something. I think Dr. Oz would have been pleased with the result of his advertorial. I've always been open to whatever experts tell me. That's what landed me here in this room near the railroad tracks of this unforgiving city.

OUR PARALLEL UNIVERSE
for Paris

When you walk towards me like someone you haven't seen for decades. When you take off your coat and hang it on the chair, apologetic for falling out of touch, your cheeks rosy from your latest excursion abroad. Stories about airport lounges and missed connections, security at every portal, a bag of rice. You had wanted to marry, it was arranged, then broken. A mishap, you explained. A new sweater and shoes from a Paris boutique, euros bulging out of your purse like lava oozing from an exploded volcano, the disarray and chaos expressing itself in spite of itself.

I could not understand your insouciance. The road was dividing like a wave, a shattering outside the cafe, screams, the chop of helicopters. Blood everywhere. I could not see our future and I was sorry about yours and what you had done to it out of spite. I wished otherwise.

The sky was falling. Shards. Particles of bone, a bent bicycle, its wheel spinning. Your body was soft against mine. I said: *It's alright, it will be over soon.*

And it was.

THE USES AND ABUSES
OF HELICOPTERS

After the briefing, the pilots talked in low tones. They had orders to scan the city for anti-aircraft weapons. This was possible because helicopters fly at low altitude, but it is also dangerous. Laser lights off the high buildings, sharp as knives. Tripwires. Propellants.

That night, the New York Mets had won the pennant and the Empire State was lit up. As soon as they were airbound, the lights began to flash: blue, orange, blue orange. Insider information, this was their signal to attack.

They retreated without injury to themselves. And the next time they went up—this time to check the weather and any movement that remained in the destroyed city—they were escorted by fighter planes and clouds.

WAR DOGS

Afterwards, when we were lying naked in the field we opened our eyes and they were there—the dogs we had trained—exploded like burst melons, all ten of them. We'd been told not to give them names. They were Canine #1, Canine #2, and so on. We were to trade off—a different dog, a different handler—every day. Our instructions were: no favorites, no attachment, no hesitation. Movement and force without sentiment, that was battlefield mantra, or some would say hypocrisy, or some would say delusion, a trick. None of the tricks worked. The dogs licked us, nuzzled us when we praised them, and they were loyal. In their last battle they had returned to save us.

MONGRELS

The mongrels have been lined up against the wall. Abject and hungry they will either be put to work or shot. Woe to those who hesitate or faint into the ditch by the side of the road. One soldier spits, then another. Townspeople—former friends—line the road behind the barricade. Some are carrying flags, others shout slogans. Children are excited by the spectacle.

An accordion player wearing cardboard shoes plays a famous tune. An old man dances as the shop fronts cast a shadow on his grinning face. One has seen him before and wondered of his origins: mongrel or pure?

Soft windy rain falls on the street and buries it in remorse.

OVENS

They are not for baking cakes or cupcakes or chickens. They do not have racks. The heat never cools. Flesh is not basted. The smoke coming out of the chimney does not smell like vanilla.

REFUGEE

Because I was tired, I took a walk to get some air. I walked into the park. It was windy. Most of the blossoms were finished, wilted or scattering in the wind. I felt lonely. I had travelled a great distance, across two oceans, across time zones. No one picked me up at the airport. There was no one to ask: How was your journey? Are you hungry? I was suddenly unable to tell time. All that I had managed so far in my life was useless to me. Remembering what they had done to my wife was the hardest. Now I was angry. Angry and alone. I felt chilled. I wanted to go home. I sat on a bench and watched a barge on the river. The water was brown, the barge was black, white and red. I was learning these words in English. Sometimes in class, I laughed with the others. But as soon as I laughed I also wanted to cry.

SEX SLAVE
for all the kidnapped girls

I am the last sex slave alive in the camp. It's almost two years later and I am grateful I have not been incinerated or died of starvation. I can hardly remember where I was before. The paths are lined with bodies, the barracks reek of excrement, sweat, spoiled food and anguish. My windows have curtains to keep out the sun and prying eyes. I spread my legs. What would you like I ask? What will give you pleasure? Sometimes they bring cake. Sometimes they bring chocolate. They allow me to bathe. They allow me to walk the perimeter of the camp. The soldier in the guard tower waves and smiles. Once, he brought me a flower. The one-eyed Commandant brings me lingerie and cooked chickens. You need sustenance he explains kindly. I don't have a schedule or an appointment book. I never know who will appear in my cottage or when. I recall, once upon a time, I was an artist.

And then when it is over and the camp is mostly quiet, I hear gunshots in the distance and then running and wild voices. And you are the first to arrive. You wrap me in blankets and take me to the field hospital. You cut my hair and examine me. Then you ask me to tell my story. I am telling you my story.

THE RE-ENACTMENT

Let's say it's early morning, cool and breezy, and the small green buds are beginning to open into figs and grapes in the arbor. The dog has been hunting and the cat is walking the parapet, slithering into danger, and you realize that for several months, maybe even years, you've played a similar role, grunting and moaning with something like desire, but more like pain—you're trying to define it—longing perhaps?

Sometimes our rational minds are out of control, wisdom suspended, all we have learned is forgotten. Our good sense, our conscience, our education, ceases to exist. We become meat.

Let's say it's an accident Let's say there's for-giveness. Let's say the weather has turned. Let's say we're afraid. Let's say we follow orders.

Then one day, our muscles strengthen. We purchase armaments.

The cave opens. All the bones of our past are buried there.

SPECIAL POWERS

Once, not so very long ago, a magician's assistant told me she could see my aura. We were visiting her Dutch stone house deep in the countryside and while my husband was interviewing her very famous magician husband for a magazine article, she took me and my five-year-old daughter to the barn to look at some paraphernalia stored in trunks. All the tricks of the trade were visible, she said, if only we chose to see them. She opened a trunk and took out a mirror, a saw, some hats, a stuffed rabbit. And, by- the- by, she said, I can see your aura. And though I knew that this, too, might be a trick, I was nearly incapacitated by this revelation. It held a power I could not resist. And the odd thing is that I cannot remember what color the aura was or what it signified. She just said she saw it and that was enough to frighten me. Maybe it was the look in her eyes; she had become a predator. I was her prey. It was like a spell and for an instant I felt faint. Then I came to and wanted to flee. I drew my daughter closer into my body, put my arm around her, held her tight, and said to the magician's assistant with the Russian name, "We'll be going now." I turned tail, literally, and walked my daughter briskly out of the barn. I opened the car door, snapped on our seat belts, revved the engine, and took off down the hard dirt driveway.

This was before the days of cell phones. I knew I'd have to return soon enough to pick up my husband. Why had he taken us along? He wanted us to have a day in the country, he had said, and magicians are, of course, fascinating people. So we went along.

I stopped at a diner and ordered some hot chocolate for my daughter and tea for me. Eventually, I calmed down. My daughter was calm, she seemed okay. I was not okay. I hadn't asked this woman to share her so-called special powers with me. Why did she presume to impose them on us?

We returned to the house and went into the parlor where the interview was taking place. The magician's assistant, who was also the magician's wife, was nowhere to be seen and that was fine with me. I told my husband that I wanted to leave, I wasn't well (a half-truth, a half-lie), and he'd have to complete the interview another time.

FIRE MEMORY

You'll be waiting for a happy ending to this story. That's why you are listening. The fire had started and there was a detour. We were on the way home after a placid weekend in the country with friends. The kids were in the back seat and they were hungry and tired. We were hungry and tired. The sky clouded over though it wasn't a cloudy day. No visibility. A cop with a flashlight a few yards ahead was barely visible. Detour, he shouted, and he pointed to his left.

There weren't many cars. We moved slowly onto a dirt road. Where are we going? my wife asked. The kids started crying. Kids are like dogs; they know. What were they sensing that we hadn't figured out?

We weren't driving away from the fire, we were driving into it.

Stupid cop, I said.

I lost sight of the car in front of us. Maybe it had turned and I hadn't noticed because suddenly we were alone on the road and the fields on either side were burning. The flames were weak and low to the ground. But what if the wind picked up? Suddenly I remembered everything I'd learned about fires when I was a volunteer forester. I remembered that if there were no trees and no wind, the fire would die out. Otherwise, we would.

THE WOMAN WITH THE TUMOR IN HER CHEEK

As soon as she gets on the train she begins to talk. The talk becomes a whine, the whine becomes a harangue.

We've all seen her many times, seen her, and looked away. The tumor is real and it's getting bigger. It's somewhere between her right upper gum and cheek, as big as an orange or a tennis ball. Her dusty blonde hair is in a ponytail and she's thin, thin as an addict. Her clothes look clean, her hair looks clean. She doesn't smell.

So what if this tumor is real and she is an addict? What then? She's carrying a translucent plastic container for money. A few dollar bills, some coins. Most of us look away. We try to read. We tell ourselves: she's an addict, don't give her money. Offer her food, ask if she knows where to get help.

Some days, I want to take her by the shoulders and heave her out of the train. Or tell her to shut up. Once, I saw four young men do this to a ranting and raving lunatic. "No one wants to listen to this shit," one of them said. They grabbed him by his shoulders and threw him out of the train. Bravo, everyone shouted, and clapped.

The train moves too slowly between stops. I begin to listen to the story about the tumor, how it's getting bigger, it won't stop growing. How if she only had money a doctor at a famous hospital would operate. How does this make sense? How is it possible that this woman wouldn't be taken care of if she walked into an emergency room? It doesn't compute.

"She's lying," I say to my neighbor who has closed his iPad and taken out his wallet.

THE HEAVY DOOR

She was tired after the interview and wondered if anyone would notice. But of course journalists always do, the wondering was useless. The next morning the headline was, "Her fatigue was evident." Who had planted this story? she asked her team. If she blamed them, fired one or two unimportant people—a secretary, a security chief—it eased her doubt. Everyone was dispensable, she told herself. Everyone.

She was known for pushing open heavy doors. Sometimes she walked around them, sometimes she slid through them like a genie in a fairy tale. Life was a fairy tale she told her closest confidantes. They listened patiently. They said nothing.

THE GIRL IN THE MIRROR
after Picasso

Once upon a time a girl looked at herself in a magic mirror. She could see her present happy childhood, her not so long ago past, and her future.

In the present and the past were her parents, the most loving mother and father in all the world. In the future was a princely husband and three children of her own. As she was still young, and not yet mature enough to marry when she first began to use the magic mirror, she preferred contemplating the future rather than the present or the past. This was understandable. But then she reached maturity, married a princely man, and had three children of her own. Even so, she only looked into the magic mirror when it reflected the future. She did not need the mirror to teach her anything about her daily life and so she avoided any troublesome reflections about her present. And as the past was past, she was not interested in it either even though memories of her idyllic childhood resided there.

Time passed and the past retreated further, the present became the past, and the future continued, for a while anyway, to stretch in front of the woman who was no longer young. Yet, as before, she did not concern herself with the past and all its consequences and discomforting thoughts. And as the past slipped away, she neglected her aging devoted parents and soon forgot them. Now when she looked into the magic mirror and saw the future, she was not pleased because her own children had forgotten her.

JEALOUSY NULLIFIED

In times of personal trouble and despair, I turn to the news. Immediately all resentment, fear and jealousy is nullified. I dream. I dream of a holiday in Canada. I dream of moving to Canada.

I arrive at mental clearings and speak only from my deepest pain. I do not hide my pain to spare my friends or family. I am a hamburger roasting on the grill charred black by forgetfulness. I have been left there while the party on the patio continues.

STORY OF REGRET
FOR VARIOUS OBJECTS

What we decided to do didn't seem so bad at the time. We stood in the living room and made lists: what to take, what to give away. It was a necessary departure, we said, and I suppose we were right, at the start anyway.

We culled, we distilled, we had a party. Someone brought balloons with the words: *Good-bye*. That didn't seem accurate. It wasn't good and it wasn't bye the bye. It was permanent, never to return. But we didn't know that at the time either.

We labeled the furniture and put the books and clothes on the bed. We told everyone to help themselves. There were discussions about this and that and then a frenzy. The greed surprised us. One or two people were embarrassed and said they had, perhaps, taken too much. They put one or two things back. We understood that it was hard to resist a giveaway, easy to forget that the giveaway was because of our getaway.

We should have done this more often, we said, ruefully. A clearing out, a reinvention. But the tears were rolling down our cheeks. Rueful was the mood of the day.

The party went on all afternoon into the night, an open house. Small children were playing underfoot and it was easier to pay attention to them, to talk about them

There was a pulped concoction in the middle of the table we could not define or describe. Meaty, but it wasn't meat. Eggplant one of our best friends said. She was trying out a new recipe that day and wanted everyone's opinion. Soon we would be gone and they'd be eating it without us at the next dinner party. Would they keep empty chairs for us like Elijah?

We had thoughts in our head we couldn't share even with each other. A plan was the safest way to express change: what time we had to leave in the morning, what time the plane would land, who would pick us up.

Years later, we remembered this party—what we'd saved, what we'd given away. And though there was only so much we could ship and carry, we knew it had been a mistake to give away our possessions before we were ready.

CONSIDERING FURNITURE

In early summer the servants covered the furniture with white sheets and packed our bags—well, the bags got packed first—and emptied the refrigerator and our mother instructed them—the servants—to have a good summer, take some time off, go to the beach, play with their children. It was up to them to lock up, shut down all the windows, turn off the lights, she told them. Because we trust you, our father said. And depend upon you, our mother said.

We waved goodbye from the back seat of our new car: two adults, two children, my brother and me. Goodbye, we waved. Goodbye. We had a chauffeur in those days, too.

That summer in Newport was like all the others. Long mornings reading on the veranda, playdates with friends, sand castles on the beach. I wasn't interested in boys yet but my brother had a girlfriend down the street and we saw very little of him. My mother didn't seem to mind. She had her own preoccupations. Our father was either playing golf, or reading, or talking to his broker on the phone.

Labor Day came and we packed and the Newport servants cleaned the house and covered the furniture with white sheets and we clambered into the back seat of the car and headed back to the city. When we arrived at the apartment sheets were still on the furniture, the house was empty of servants and smelled of smoke. Our parents were silent; they never showed much emotion. There'd been a fire in the building next door and they hadn't heard a word. All our furniture was ruined.

PERFECT WEATHER

We've been waiting for perfect weather. It's finally arrived. The sun is out, the temperature is temperate, there's no prospect of rain in the hours ahead, and though the word "cloudy" is in the forecast, we've decided to risk a journey to the seashore to collect shells and soak in some sun after a long, hard, endless winter. Of course, it wasn't really endless because here we are and the weather is perfect today, it's spring at last. And if we continue to postpone our outing to the seashore, it will never happen, will it? We can't rely on the weather or plan around the weather all the time especially if the forecast is uncertain, as it often is. But that is exactly what we've been doing lately—postponing and postponing and postponing.

From time to time I have imagined a solution to our weather problem: we could move. If we moved to another city in another state, or even a city in another country, the weather problem we have where we live now would not exist.

THE POET

The well-known poet got up onto the stage to read his work. There was a large audience, his fans filled the room. He brought the microphone very close to his mouth. His words were percussive, angry. Yet he was reciting—more like declaiming I should say—a seasonal poem.

Months earlier, when I had been arranging the schedule of events at the café, I had asked the well-known poet if he would agree to share the evening with a younger, less established poet. He had agreed. At the time, I hadn't picked up on his reluctance. Unlike his work, it was subtle, or maybe I didn't know him very well, or at all, for that matter. I only knew his work—which I liked—and his reputation as a gadfly, which had nothing to do with me. I am not a poet, I am the manager of a café. I suppose he understood that if he refused, I would not put him on the schedule, he'd have to find another venue.

The trouble started two weeks before the reading. I invited him to a rehearsal —we wanted to time the reading—and he didn't get back to me for several days. When he finally did call, he said he'd have to ask his wife. He wasn't married so I laughed. "I don't need a rehearsal," he said. "I'm good at timing myself and I like to decide on the spot what I will read. I feel the mood in the room."

Meanwhile, the young, less-established poet, was getting more and more nervous. And so was I because I'd invited the press.

He stayed on the stage for a very long time, well beyond his limit, which was twenty minutes, long enough for any poet. On and on he went, spitting and declaiming into the microphone. People were holding their ears, people were walking out. I wish I could have done the same.

3. SALAMANDERS
IN MY POCKETS

DOGS WELCOME

A friend from college is getting married. Children are not invited to the wedding. It's on Long Island, a real bitch to get to, not that she considered anyone's travel challenges when she booked the venue. "They allow dogs," she told me. What does that mean? Dogs are invited but children aren't? That's a paraphrase of my impatient question. Why can't this high-powered lawyer friend of mine connect her own dots?

I don't want to go, my husband doesn't want to go, my daughter wouldn't have cared less if I'd mentioned it to her, which I didn't. The question is: should I boycott this wedding, insult my friend, and probably say sayonara to the friendship.

In the end what does it all matter? The other day on 60 minutes, one of my favorite programs, Michael Caine, who had just turned 82, said: "I don't know how I got here." That was a sad statement. Had he been sleeping all his life?

My friend is like that, too. She doesn't know how she got anywhere.

So I've made a decision: I will leave my husband and daughter behind and go to the wedding with our dog. After all, dogs are welcome.

THE $5,000 NECKLACE

There was no emotion attached to the revelation: the necklace was missing. We were walking on the street side-by-side. Her face was in profile, the street crowded and noisy. Had I misunderstood? "I thought it would turn up again as I was packing for this move," she said.

"You owned a necklace worth $5,000?"

"Yes, I bought it as a present for myself in Paris."

As friendships go, I had known this woman for a long time. She always dressed modestly: good fabrics, conventional cuts, no loud colors. Her taste in entertainment and books was the same. Nothing out of the ordinary. Early to bed, early to rise, nothing unexpected at work or play. But she was single—no partner of either gender for all the years I'd known her, no dating that she talked about. And all her friends, including me, had wondered about her reclusiveness. "What explains our friend's odd life?" we whispered to each other in our more gossipy moods.

"Did you lose it or was it stolen?" I asked.

"I don't know."

"Was it insured?"

"No."

There were now three announcements to process: the necklace itself, its loss, and the fact that it hadn't been insured.

"This is unprecedented," I said. "I did not realize..."

We had arrived at the subway station, said goodnight, and went our separate ways to different trains. She would be leaving the city for good in a few days. And that did not seem to matter to her either.

DOPPLEGANGER

A woman approached me on the pool deck. "Hi, Jan. It's good to see you. We missed you in class today."

She was an instructor I have seen working in the warm, small pool for babies and "the elderly" many times. Her particular class is for women of a certain age who have stiff joints. She plays loud, funky music and was toting her boom box. Class was over and I'd missed it!

I may be a woman of a certain age, but I am a lap swimmer who once upon a time was a competitive swimmer. And my joints may be stiff, but I pay no attention. I don't take classes and I had never talked to this instructor before.

So her approach to me was weird. "I don't take any classes," I told her.

That startled her. "Oh my, and your name is Jan? You have a Doppelgänger. Another Jan, similar build."

I didn't like this story, it made me uncomfortable. Not only did this Doppelgänger look like me, she had the same name.

I don't want a "twin" who is unrelated. But I was also intrigued, albeit eerily so. In mythology—German, Norse, Egyptian—a Doppelgänger is an evil twin and harbinger of bad luck or death. No thank you.

I stuck with my intuition and didn't take my inquiry further. I got into the pool and had a good swim.

DR. PHIL, MY INNER CHILD AND ME

Dr. Phil recommends that we take care of our inner child so I have decided to bring her with me to his show. A friend gave me free tickets. I am very excited to see this great man in person. I am hoping that if I raise my hand, he will call on me.

My inner child is wearing a light blue dress with long sleeves. Her dark black hair is curly and thick. She's three-years-old and very talkative.

The topic of today's show is obedience and defying authority. That's complicated for a three-year-old so I plan to interpret as Dr. Phil speaks.

I settle into my seat and put my inner child on my lap. No one sees her, of course, but I know she is there. She is heavy and fidgety. I ask her to calm down but she doesn't calm down.

Two grownups are on the stage talking about their disobedient children. They seem mean and impatient just like my parents. I disobeyed them and left home when I was sixteen. I never finished high school and now I have a low-level job and an inner child to take care of. It's no fun.

I raise my hand and Dr. Phil calls on me. I like his voice. He's handsome in person and he's tall, very tall. He stands up when he talks to me. I ask a question and he is kind when he answers. He praises my concern for my inner child who is very disobedient. He suggests I come backstage and talk to him after the show. I'm thrilled. Maybe he'll give me his autograph.

I AM OFFERED A PRODUCT

"All I want to do is deposit this check," I tell the young man whose name is Louis, according to the label on his wrinkled white shirt.

"Today is your lucky day because the bank is offering a special product. And you have been pre-approved, your credit is good," Louis says.

I've arrived at an off-hour, my intention, I hate lines and waiting, and here I am waylaid by a sales pitch by Louis, the teller, who I had thought was employed to take my deposit, hand me cash, or help me solve a discrepancy on my statement.

I've handed him my check with the deposit slip but he still hasn't processed it. I look at my watch. Three minutes.

He's very friendly and has a sweet face and he's young, so I am trying to be patient. Five minutes.

"Louis, listen, I'm not here to purchase anything, I'm here to deposit a check. It's a simple transaction."

"This is a really good deal. If you spend $500 in a month you get $200 back."

"How does that work?"

I've asked a question. Big mistake.

Seven minutes.

"Look I can fill out this form, right here, right now."

"Sure, do it, Louis. Let's be done with this. I'm hungry. I need to get some lunch. Do me a favor and tell your boss that you are no longer a teller, you're a salesman. And a good one."

THE DALAI LAMA IS
A FRIEND OF MINE

And have I mentioned that I meet him in the locker room at the gym. Of course he is never alone; he has an entourage. He enters in his saffron robes but discards them. He chats easily. He smiles. He guffaws.

His doctors—more than one—have suggested a regimen and he must obey (guffaw). He is handed shorts and a tank top. He is fleshy I notice, his muscles are flaccid. "I see you are well formed," he says.

"I work-out a lot," I reply.

"And how do you find it?"

"Congenial," I reply.

Now he chortles—a lighter laugh than a guffaw—and sits down on the bench to put on exercise shorts on top of his boxer shorts. (Yes, the Dalai Lama wears boxer shorts.)

"And now the tank top," he says. "We had a wonderful shopping spree in Modell's."

He leans over me and puts his hand on my bare shoulder. It is calloused which surprises me. I have always thought of the Dalai Lama as a baby, like Jesus in the manger. But he is a grown fleshy man, a mere mortal, like me.

THE SEVEN FOOT MAN WITH
THE SMALL HEAD

The seven foot man with the small head came into the locker room. I wasn't sure at first if he was a potato with a stalk or a person. But then another reporter arrived and he introduced me to the seven foot man. He said, "I think the two of you will have a lot in common. The only problem is, I don't know how old he is."

I decided to ask as soon as we were introduced. "How old are you?"

"Four, the big man said."

The locker room was a *cul de sac,* too small for a seven foot man trying to put on his street clothes after a game. His limbs stretched from one end of the bench to the other. Reporters were crowded all around him. He'd made a lot of baskets and won the game for his team.

I wasn't interested in all of that. I wanted to go out with him. I was the only female reporter in the room. Lucky me! And I liked the seven foot man with the small head. He was jolly and friendly.

I asked him if he'd like to go out for a drink. He said, sure, at least I think that is what he said. His head was too far away for me to hear him clearly, as small and distant as a galaxy in another universe.

YOU SHOULD NOT PUSH THE ELEVATOR BUTTON

Because you have entered the elevator, quite naturally you want to push the button. You do not think for a minute that the two other people in the elevator have already pushed the button. Note: you are all going down to the lobby. Now there are three people who have pushed the L button.

Because no one is talking there is no com-munication about buttons or where the elevator is going because, obviously, it is going down. Perhaps no one trusts that the button is working, or that the elevator is, in fact, going down, or that it will arrive safely

At first, when you began to notice this quirk in every human who enters the elevator, you assumed it was only office workers in very tall buildings who pushed the L button. But even in your small, friendly building, everyone pushes the L button. First they say hello or good morning and then they push the button even though they know, as you know, that someone who has entered the elevator before them has pushed the button. You seem relieved when a dog enters the elevator. Dogs do not push buttons though, undoubtedly, they trust their owners to push it for them.

OTHER PEOPLE'S DREAMS

"I had a very interesting dream last night," he says.

All the chatter stops, we must be polite, he is our host, we are captive.

Has he gathered us for the very purpose of reciting his dream? Would he like to hear ours? Does he expect commentary? Interpretation? Once I tried to recite my own dream but he cut me off and asked if anyone would like some dessert.

NARCISSISM: SOME EXAMPLES

Instead of asking, how are you doing, you tell me how you are doing.

Instead of asking, how are your spirits after your difficult year—we haven't seen each other in a year—you begin a recitation of all your recent travels, your daughter's engagement, and the brilliance of your new boyfriend. I think "dogged" is the word you use to describe him, meaning that he can solve any problem, and does.

Instead of asking what can I do for you as a friend right now, you complain about a mutual friend's snarky comment to which I cannot respond without being disloyal. But that is the point: you want me to be disloyal to her and loyal only to you.

Instead of complimenting me on my strength, you tell me about a dear friend with Parkinson's who is stronger than anyone you know, mostly because of your ministrations, for which he is eternally grateful.

Oddly, you ask about my husband. Do I have a recent picture? Whereupon you pull out your iPhone to show me pictures of your new boyfriend, your new condo in New Orleans, and your daughter's handsome fiancé.

Instead of asking how my daughter is doing, you ask about her hair. Is it long or short? Then you tell me about your new hair stylist.

Finally, you ask about a concert I played the other night which you could not attend because you were attending to yourself. How did it go? Whereupon you pull out a DVD of a recital you played in Venice. Would I like a copy, you ask, as you hand it to me. Although it was many years ago, you have not forgotten the applause.

AT THE NAIL SALON

I decided to get a pedicure. My nails were very long, it was summer, time for sandals. My wife said, "They are disgusting, you are piercing my shins in bed, how do you expect me to play footsie with you?"

I had been to my wife's preferred nail salon once before when we went for an anniversary his/her manicure/pedicure. We sat next to each other and vibrated our chairs. We chatted to the workers: mine was from Ecuador, hers was from China. "How long have you been here?" is the usual opening question. Usually, they don't understand or pretend not to understand. Mostly, they're illegal, we get that, but chatting passes the time. Also, enjoying the knee-ankle massage, the vibrating chair, browsing through women's magazines, or checking email.

This time, I had my wife's Chinese worker. She was wearing a jade bracelet on one arm and either a Fitbit or an Apple watch on the other. Maybe she owned the salon, I thought, because these watches are expensive. I wanted to clarify the kind of watch and her relationship to the salon. I wanted her to notice me. I'd heard her talking in English as well as Chinese. She was completely bi-lingual, maybe even born in New York.

"Is that a Fitbit or an Apple watch?" I asked. Then I pointed to the less expensive Fitbit on my arm.

"What do you think of it?" I continued.

She hadn't been looking at me or my disgusting feet; she'd been looking up, around, talking in Chinese to a compadre. Now she looked at me. It was a look of disdain: how dare I interrupt her private reverie or inquire about her watch? She dropped my left foot back into the water and walked away. Five minutes later, another woman took her place.

"Where are you from originally?" I began.

"No understand English," was the reply.

PREFACE TO THE CLOUD SPOTTER'S GUIDE TO THE UNIVERSE

If you've loved looking at clouds, this book is for you. And if you've never noticed clouds, perhaps this book will inspire you to do so.

A few years ago I decided to look at clouds in a new way. I went to the park and sat on a bench for about an hour. I studied the river, the trees, the flowers, the boats on the river, and the leaves on the trees. Then I looked up. After a while I couldn't see anything but the sky and the clouds. I took out my iPhone and snapped some pictures. Clouds are very photogenic.

I don't worry about remembering their Latin names: cumulus, cirrocumulus, lenticularis, etc. These were invented by professional cloud spotters and scientists. I am an amateur.

Where does a cloud begin and where does it end? Where does it come from and where does it go? Did cave men and cave women tell stories about clouds? When did they first appear in our atmosphere? Do all the planets—those we know about and those still unknown—have clouds in their atmosphere?

Arriving at these questions is like learning a new song. So let's sing it.

AN INTERVIEW WITH THE AUTHOR

Q: I'd like to discuss the entire NOMADS trilogy if you don't mind. How did you begin? Is it finished?

A: I began in 2000 when I was working on "Another Day in Paradise," a book about international humanitarian workers. I compiled, edited the book, and ghosted some of the stories. It took two years and it was engrossing, very intense. I had to travel a bit and work with many stories about war, atrocities and natural disasters.

In order to keep myself grounded while working on the "Another Day" project, I began to sketch small stories. It was all I had time to do for myself in between the traveling, interviewing and editing.

Q: Why did you decide to collect these stories and publish them?

A: I showed a few to writer friends and they com-mented on the precision of the writing, the unusual genre I'd chosen (similar to Lydia Davis, they said), and the experimental feel of the work—not fact, not fiction, something new and different for me—as I either write journalism, blogs, or dedicated fiction.

So I decided to write more short short stories and see what happened. It was an exploration, a writing discipline. What is fact and what is fiction? Do we always have to disclaim when we are not writing journalism? My view is that if we mess with the facts we are creating factoids (a Norman Mailer word) and therefore we are totally in the realm of fiction. I certainly tell my nonfiction students to be careful—not to conflate or fabricate.

NOMADS are fictions and understanding that, accepting it, gave me freedom.

Titles began to accumulate in my journal. Before long I had enough pieces for the first volume.

Q: Why did you decide to use actors for the launch of the first and second NOMADS at the Cornelia Street Café? Will you be using actors for the launch of Nomads3?

A: It happened serendipitously. I reconnected with my daughter's long-ago babysitter, Stephanie Stone. She's an actor. I had moved into Stephanie's neighborhood and we would walk and talk on Saturday mornings. She invited me to a poetry reading—all actors reading well-known poems. The actors' expression evoked new interpretations. And, of course, they are articulate and can project.

So I said to Stephanie, "What if I had a launch and I sat in the audience and you read my work?" We rehearsed an evening with two other actor/directors: Constance George and Burke Walker. I am grateful to all of them. They told me that many of the stories read like monologues. Some even have dialogue and were read by two of the actors.

Most importantly, to hear my work read and re-interpreted by the actors was an exciting experience for me. It changed the way I wrote the pieces for Nomads 2 and Nomads 3. I sometimes hear them "spoken." I'd taken a playwriting class—and failed dismally. The actors did well but I didn't; my instinct is always to write narrative prose. I came up with ideas but couldn't get anything to work using dialogue. Now I think the class did have a delayed effect. Maybe I'll eventually be able to write a "play." I think Richard Caliban, my playwriting teacher at Gotham Writers Workshop, would be pleased.

And, yes, I will launch Nomads 3 using actors to read a selection of stories.

Q. Is the NOMADS series finished?

A. I think it is—mostly—because I want to get on to other things. And once I have that desire, I know I am done. Most writers move into new projects with ease; we rarely look back. And though I am calling NOMADS a trilogy because I wrote each book over time, my sense is that it is all one work, and that it is finished.

www.ingramcontent.com/pod-product-compliance
Lightning Source LLC
Chambersburg PA
CBHW071641050426
42443CB00026B/847